# No Night-Night

## A Bedtime Story in English and American Sign Language

Zena Bailey-Harris

To my wonderful mother, Aslee E. Bailey, with all my love and admiration. And in loving memory of my father, James L. Bailey.

"The things that make me different are the things that make me."

—Winnie the Pooh

## Mountain Arbor Press

Alpharetta, GA

Copyright © 2018 by Action Items, LLC

All rights reserved. No part of this book may be reproduced or transmitted in any form or by any means, electronic or mechanical, including photocopying, recording, or any information storage and retrieval system, without permission in writing from the author.

ISBN: 978-1-63183-246-8

Library of Congress Control Number: 2018936233

10 9 8 7 6 5 4 3 2          0 4 0 7 1 8

Printed in the United States of America

∞ This paper meets the requirements of ANSI/NISO Z39.48-1992 (Permanence of Paper)

Illustrations by Najah Clemmons

# Introduction

*Two children meet on a playground. One child waves a silent but friendly "hello" to the other . . . and the fun begins. They chase each other from the slides to the swings and play a robust game of hide-and-seek before resting on a bench. One child finally introduces herself, then says, "What's your name?" The other child lifts a hand and starts to fingerspell. The hearing child tries hard to understand, but she can't quite get the name right. So, the deaf child reaches into a bag and pulls out a book: on one page, there is American Sign Language (ASL), and on the opposite page, standard English. As the two children sit side by side reading this book, soon they come to understand each other. The language barrier is slowly eroded . . . and a friendship begins!*

If you have a heart for deaf children like I do, you may have Googled, Binged, and physically searched bookstores for a storybook in American Sign Language (ASL) for deaf children. Finding nothing, I decided to write one myself!

This story is written in English and ASL. The English prose and illustrations are shown first on the left, and the ASL translation is pictured on the opposite page. I've provided labels for each sign for the convenience of native English speakers and emerging signers. Following are a few facts about ASL that readers new to the language will find helpful.

• ASL is a visual language. Facial expressions, intensity, and directionality are important elements of ASL grammar that are easier to convey in live action. Additionally, it is subjective. Two people given the same English sentence will each sign it differently, and both could be correct.

• ASL does not follow English word order. For example, the sentence "I ate my dinner" is signed as "Dinner finish." The sign for dinner is made with two signs: eat + night.

• All children love to have someone read to them. This book was written to entertain all children, especially those who are deaf and hard of hearing. *No Night-Night* is a book all their own that they can identify with, learn from, and share as they learn to navigate communication in a hearing world.

It is my hope that parents, children, and all interested parties enjoy this story. Moreover, my dream is that *No Night-Night* helps to bridge the language gap between hearing and deaf children. After all, kids are kids. No one should be made to feel different, isolated, or misunderstood simply because they cannot hear.

Finally, here are a few great resources for ASL vocabulary and grammar:

- Lifeprint.com
- Signingsavvy.com
- Youtube.com
- CATS Library at www.cats.gatech.edu

Please enjoy *No Night-Night: A Bedtime Story in English and American Sign Language*!

all day

play

me

And part of the night.

night

play

continue

I ate my dinner...

dinner

finish

pah

night

clothes

my

favorite

yay

 with

 Mommy

 sit on

 rocking chair

 cuddle

Before I know it . . .

Soon

I'm closing my eyes . . .

eyes closing

I guess

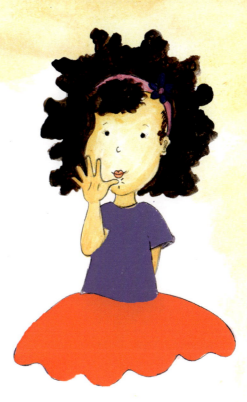
Mommy

right